2021 2022

The Original STUDENT CALENDAR

August 2, 2021 *to* September 4, 2022

Name: ______________________

Address: ______________________

____

Phone: ______________________

email: ______________________

POLESTAR CALENDARS

www.polestarcalendars.com ★ 1-800-296-6955

THE ORIGINAL STUDENT CALENDAR
August 2021 — August 2022

ISBN 978-1-55186-119-7
(x nóta 978-1-55186-124-1)

Edited by Julian Ross

Cover design by Emanuel Smedbøl emanuel.smedbol.ca
Production and layout by Gillian Stead

THE ORIGINAL STUDENT CALENDAR – 39th Edition!

Published and created in Canada by:
Polestar Calendars Ltd.,
6518 Slocan River Road, Winlaw, B.C., Canada V0G 2J0
Phone/fax: 1-800-296-6955 email: info@polestarcalendars.com
www.polestarcalendars.com

and distributed in the United States by:
Orca Book Publishers, 1-800-210-5277

We also publish the *Polestar Business Agenda*, a complete time-management system for your working life; the *Polestar Planner*, a personal organizer and the *Polestar Family Calendar*, a calendar that's perfect for the whole family. For more info, visit our website www.polestarcalendars.com.

FSC www.fsc.org
MIX
Paper from responsible sources
FSC® C103567

This agenda is made of material from well-managed FSC®-certified forests, recycled materials and other controlled sources.

Welcome!

Thanks for buying this edition of **THE ORIGINAL STUDENT CALENDAR.** We appreciate your support and sincerely hope that it serves your needs well. Features include:

- an easy-to-use three-part time management format
- lots of room to write in each day
- month-at-a-glance pages for the whole year
- term timetables plus telephone and address pages
- space to record your courses, test and essay results
- a place to record your goals, dreams & accomplishments
- monthly budget/expense pages at the back
- plus blank pages for notes

and it's all designed to help make your life as a student more organized and more enjoyable.

To keep your place in the calendar during the year, you can tear off the bottom page perforations. Also, there are pockets for notes, receipts, etc. at the front and back of the calendar.

We really welcome your feedback, so if you've got any suggestions, please let us know. Thanks, and we hope you have a great year.

Time Management Format:

Each day is divided into three sections: *Appointments & Assignments, General Study,* and *The Rest of Your Life*. In the first section, *Appointments & Assignments*, you mark the *due date* of all assignments or tests, plus all your *appointments*. In the second section, *General Study*, you write down *when* you're going to *prepare* those assignments and *study* for those tests, so you can have some free time left to enjoy all the things you've written down in section three, *The Rest Of Your Life*.

APPOINTMENTS & ASSIGNMENTS	GENERAL STUDY	THE REST OF YOUR LIFE
10:00 Fiction 302	7:45 – 9:30 a.m. finish Esi Edugyan essay	do some laundry!
by 1 = English Lit essay due for Dr. Morris	1 – 3:15 Linguistics lab	5: 30 soccer
3:30 – 4:30 study Accounting	4:30 – 5 look into Co-op Abroad options	8 – meet writing group in SUB

TERM TIMETABLE

THE ORIGINAL STUDENT CALENDAR

TERM TIMETABLE

MORNING

AFTERNOON

	Monday	*Tuesday*	*Wednesday*	*Thursday*	*Friday*	*Saturday*	*Sunday*
7:30 A.M.							
8:00							
8:30							
9:00							
9:30							
10:00							
10:30							
11:00							
11:30							
12:00 P.M.							
12:30							
1:00							
1:30							
2:00							
2:30							

AFTERNOON

EVENING

	Monday	*Tuesday*	*Wednesday*	*Thursday*	*Friday*	*Saturday*	*Sunday*
3:00							
3:30							
4:00							
4:30							
5:00							
5:30							
6:00							
6:30							
7:00							
7:30							
8:00							
8:30							
9:00							
9:30							
10:00							
10:30							

TERM TIMETABLE **THE ORIGINAL STUDENT CALENDAR** **TERM TIMETABLE**

	Monday	*Tuesday*	*Wednesday*	*Thursday*	*Friday*	*Saturday*	*Sunday*
7:30 A.M.							
8:00							
8:30							
9:00							
9:30							
10:00							
10:30							
11:00							
11:30							
12:00 P.M.							
12:30							
1:00							
1:30							
2:00							
2:30							

MORNING

AFTERNOON

AFTERNOON

EVENING

	Monday	Tuesday	Wednesday	Thursday	Friday	Saturday	Sunday
3:00							
3:30							
4:00							
4:30							
5:00							
5:30							
6:00							
6:30							
7:00							
7:30							
8:00							
8:30							
9:00							
9:30							
10:00							
10:30							

TERM TIMETABLE — # THE ORIGINAL STUDENT CALENDAR — **TERM TIMETABLE**

MORNING

AFTERNOON

	Monday	*Tuesday*	*Wednesday*	*Thursday*	*Friday*	*Saturday*	*Sunday*
7:30 A.M.							
8:00							
8:30							
9:00							
9:30							
10:00							
10:30							
11:00							
11:30							
12:00 P.M.							
12:30							
1:00							
1:30							
2:00							
2:30							

AFTERNOON

EVENING

	Monday	Tuesday	Wednesday	Thursday	Friday	Saturday	Sunday
3:00							
3:30							
4:00							
4:30							
5:00							
5:30							
6:00							
6:30							
7:00							
7:30							
8:00							
8:30							
9:00							
9:30							
10:00							
10:30							

THE ORIGINAL STUDENT CALENDAR

Course / #	Course Goals	Room # / Location
Class Times	Class Times	Class Times
Professor – Email/phone	Office # / Office Hours	Teaching Assistant
Date	Test/Assignment	Mark or Percentage

Course / #	Course Goals	Room # / Location
Class Times	Class Times	Class Times
Professor – Email/phone	Office # / Office Hours	Teaching Assistant
Date	Test/Assignment	Mark or Percentage

Course / #	Course Goals	Room # / Location
Class Times	Class Times	Class Times
Professor – Email/phone	Office # / Office Hours	Teaching Assistant
Date	Test/Assignment	Mark or Percentage

Course / #	Course Goals	Room # / Location
Class Times	Class Times	Class Times
Professor – Email/phone	Office # / Office Hours	Teaching Assistant
Date	Test/Assignment	Mark or Percentage

COURSES & MARKS

Course / #	Course Goals	Room # / Location
Class Times	Class Times	Class Times
Professor – Email/phone	Office # / Office Hours	Teaching Assistant

Date	Test/Assignment	Mark or Percentage

Course / #	Course Goals	Room # / Location
Class Times	Class Times	Class Times
Professor – Email/phone	Office # / Office Hours	Teaching Assistant

Date	Test/Assignment	Mark or Percentage

Course / #	Course Goals	Room # / Location
Class Times	Class Times	Class Times
Professor – Email/phone	Office # / Office Hours	Teaching Assistant
Date	Test/Assignment	Mark or Percentage

Course / #	Course Goals	Room # / Location
Class Times	Class Times	Class Times
Professor – Email/phone	Office # / Office Hours	Teaching Assistant
Date	Test/Assignment	Mark or Percentage

Course / #	Course Goals	Room # / Location
Class Times	Class Times	Class Times
Professor – Email/phone	Office # / Office Hours	Teaching Assistant
Date	Test/Assignment	Mark or Percentage

Course / #	Course Goals	Room # / Location
Class Times	Class Times	Class Times
Professor – Email/phone	Office # / Office Hours	Teaching Assistant
Date	Test/Assignment	Mark or Percentage

Course / #	Course Goals	Room # / Location
Class Times	Class Times	Class Times
Professor – Email/phone	Office # / Office Hours	Teaching Assistant
Date	Test/Assignment	Mark or Percentage

Course / #	Course Goals	Room # / Location
Class Times	Class Times	Class Times
Professor – Email/phone	Office # / Office Hours	Teaching Assistant
Date	Test/Assignment	Mark or Percentage

AUGUST 2021 THE ORIGINAL STUDENT CALENDAR **AUGUST 2021**

Sunday	Monday	Tuesday	Wednesday	Thursday	Friday	Saturday
1	2 *Civic Holiday (Canada)*	3	4	5	6	7
8 ● *New Moon*	9	10	11	12	13	14
15	16	17	18	19	20	21
22 ○ *Full Moon*	23	24	25	26	27	28
29	30	31				

SEPTEMBER 2021 **THE ORIGINAL STUDENT CALENDAR** SEPTEMBER 2021

Sunday	Monday	Tuesday	Wednesday	Thursday	Friday	Saturday
			1	2	3	4
5	6 *Labour Day, ● New Moon*	7 *First day of Rosh Hashanah*	8	9	10	11
12	13	14	15	16 *Yom Kippur*	17	18
19	20 *○ Full Moon*	21 *U.N. International Day of Peace*	22 *Autumnal Equinox*	23	24	25
26	27	28	29	30		

OCTOBER 2021 THE ORIGINAL STUDENT CALENDAR OCTOBER 2021

Sunday	Monday	Tuesday	Wednesday	Thursday	Friday	Saturday
					1	2
3	4	5	6 ● *New Moon*	7	8	9
10	11 *Thanksgiving Day (Canada), Columbus Day (U.S.)*	12	13	14	15	16
17	18	19	20 ○ *Full Moon*	21	22	23
24 / *Halloween* 31	25	26	27	28	29	30

 THE ORIGINAL STUDENT CALENDAR NOVEMBER 2021

Sunday	Monday	Tuesday	Wednesday	Thursday	Friday	Saturday
	1	2	3	4 *Diwali, ● New Moon*	5	6
7 *Daylight Saving Time ends (set clock back one hour)*	8	9	10	11 *Remembrance Day (Canada), Veterans' Day (U.S.)*	12	13
14	15	16	17	18	19 *○ Full Moon*	20 *Universal Children's Day*
21	22	23	24	25 *Thanksgiving Day (U.S.)*	26	27
28	29 *First day of Hanukkah*	30				

THE ORIGINAL STUDENT CALENDAR

DECEMBER 2021

Sunday	Monday	Tuesday	Wednesday	Thursday	Friday	Saturday
			1	2	3 ● *New Moon*	4
5	6	7	8	9	10	11
12	13	14	15	16	17	18 ○ *Full Moon*
19	20	21 *Winter Solstice*	22	23	24	25 *Christmas Day*
26 *Boxing Day (Canada)*	27	28	29	30	31 *New Year's Eve*	

THE ORIGINAL STUDENT CALENDAR

JANUARY 2022

Sunday	Monday	Tuesday	Wednesday	Thursday	Friday	Saturday
						1 *New Year's Day*
2 ● *New Moon*	3	4	5	6	7	8
9	10	11	12	13	14	15
16	17 *Martin Luther King, Jr. Day (U.S.),* ○ *Full Moon*	18	19	20	21	22
23 / 30	24 / ● *New Moon* 31	25	26	27	28	29

FEBRUARY 2022 **THE ORIGINAL STUDENT CALENDAR** FEBRUARY 2022

Sunday	Monday	Tuesday	Wednesday	Thursday	Friday	Saturday
		1 *Chinese New Year (Year of the Tiger)*	2 *Groundhog Day*	3	4	5
6	7	8	9	10	11	12
13	14 *Valentine's Day*	15	16 ○ *Full Moon*	17	18	19
20	21 *Family/Heritage Day (Canada), Presidents' Day (U.S.)*	22	23	24	25	26
27	28					

MARCH 2022 **THE ORIGINAL STUDENT CALENDAR** MARCH 2022

Sunday	Monday	Tuesday	Wednesday	Thursday	Friday	Saturday
		1	2 *Ash Wednesday, ● New Moon*	3	4	5
6	7	8 *International Women's Day*	9	10	11	12
13 *Daylight Saving Time begins (set clock ahead one hour)*	14	15	16	17 *Purim, St. Patrick's Day*	18 *○ Full Moon*	19 *Holi*
20 *Vernal Equinox*	21	22	23	24	25	26
27	28	29	30	31		

THE ORIGINAL STUDENT CALENDAR

APRIL 2022

Sunday	Monday	Tuesday	Wednesday	Thursday	Friday	Saturday
					1 ● *New Moon*	2
3 *First day of Ramadam*	4	5	6	7	8	9
10 *Palm Sunday*	11	12	13	14	15 *Good Friday*	16 *First day of Passover,* ○ *Full Moon*
17 *Easter*	18	19	20	21	22 *Earth Day*	23
24	25	26	27	28	29	30 ● *New Moon*

MAY 2022

THE ORIGINAL STUDENT CALENDAR

MAY 2022

Sunday	Monday	Tuesday	Wednesday	Thursday	Friday	Saturday
1	2	3	4	5	6	7
8 *Mother's Day (Canada, U.S.)*	9	10	11	12	13	14
15 ○ *Full Moon*	16	17	18	19	20	21
22	23 *Victoria Day (Canada)*	24	25	26	27	28
29	30 *Memorial Day (U.S.),* ● *New Moon*	31				

THE ORIGINAL STUDENT CALENDAR

JUNE 2022

Sunday	Monday	Tuesday	Wednesday	Thursday	Friday	Saturday
			1	2	3	4
5	6	7	8	9	10	11
12	13	14 ○ *Full Moon*	15	16	17	18
19 *Father's Day (Canada, U.S.)*	20	21 *National Indigenous Peoples Day (Canada), Summer Solstice*	22	23	24 *St. Jean Baptiste Day (Canada)*	25
26	27	28 ● *New Moon*	29	30		

JULY 2022

THE ORIGINAL STUDENT CALENDAR

JULY 2022

Sunday	*Monday*	*Tuesday*	*Wednesday*	*Thursday*	*Friday*	*Saturday*
					1 *Canada Day*	2
3	4 *Independence Day (U.S.)*	5	6	7	8	9
10	11	12	13 ○ *Full Moon*	14	15	16
17	18	19	20	21	22	23
24 / 31	25	26	27	28 ● *New Moon*	29	30

AUGUST 2022 # THE ORIGINAL STUDENT CALENDAR **AUGUST 2022**

Sunday	Monday	Tuesday	Wednesday	Thursday	Friday	Saturday
	1 *Civic Holiday (Canada)*	2	3	4	5	6
7	8	9	10	11 ○ *Full Moon*	12	13
14	15	16	17	18	19	20
21	22	23	24	25	26	27 ● *New Moon*
28	29	30	31			

THE ORIGINAL STUDENT CALENDAR

*2021-2022: Goals, Dreams & Accomplishments**

** Use this page to plan and prepare for the coming year. Consider all your goals and objectives – i.e. academic, personal, athletic, etc. To help maintain your focus, you might want to look at and update it throughout the year. For privacy, you might want to tear this page out and keep in your room or in a private place.*

THE ORIGINAL STUDENT CALENDAR

AUGUST 2021						
S	M	T	W	T	F	S
1	**2**	**3**	**4**	**5**	**6**	**7**
8	9	10	11	12	13	14
15	16	17	18	19	20	21
22	23	24	25	26	27	28
29	30	31				

TO DO THIS WEEK

APPOINTMENTS & ASSIGNMENTS	GENERAL STUDY	THE REST OF YOUR LIFE
Monday, Aug. 2 *Civic Holiday (Canada)*		
Tuesday, Aug. 3		
Wednesday, Aug. 4		

THE ORIGINAL STUDENT CALENDAR

TO DO THIS MONTH	
	The future begins now. — *Andrei Tarkovsky*

APPOINTMENTS & ASSIGNMENTS	GENERAL STUDY	THE REST OF YOUR LIFE
Thursday, Aug. 5		
Friday, Aug. 6		

Saturday, Aug. 7	Sunday, Aug. 8 ● *New Moon*

THE ORIGINAL STUDENT CALENDAR

AUGUST 2021						
S	M	T	W	T	F	S
1	**2**	3	4	5	6	7
8	**9**	**10**	**11**	**12**	**13**	**14**
15	16	17	18	19	20	21
22	23	24	25	26	27	28
29	30	31				

TO DO THIS WEEK

APPOINTMENTS & ASSIGNMENTS	GENERAL STUDY	THE REST OF YOUR LIFE
Monday, Aug. 9		
Tuesday, Aug. 10		
Wednesday, Aug. 11		

THE ORIGINAL STUDENT CALENDAR

TO DO THIS MONTH	
	Nothing's impossible. It's what you decide your limits are. — *Lori Ann Muenzer*

APPOINTMENTS & ASSIGNMENTS	GENERAL STUDY	THE REST OF YOUR LIFE
Thursday, Aug. 12		
Friday, Aug. 13		

Saturday, Aug. 14	Sunday, Aug. 15

THE ORIGINAL STUDENT CALENDAR

AUGUST 2021						
S	M	T	W	T	F	S
1	**2**	3	4	5	6	7
8	9	10	11	12	13	14
15	**16**	**17**	**18**	**19**	**20**	**21**
22	23	24	25	26	27	28
29	30	31				

TO DO THIS WEEK

APPOINTMENTS & ASSIGNMENTS	GENERAL STUDY	THE REST OF YOUR LIFE
Monday, Aug. 16		
Tuesday, Aug. 17		
Wednesday, Aug. 18		

THE ORIGINAL STUDENT CALENDAR

TO DO THIS MONTH

The secret to life is to put yourself in the right lighting. For some, it's a Broadway spotlight; for others, a lamplit desk.

— *Susan Cain*

APPOINTMENTS & ASSIGNMENTS	GENERAL STUDY	THE REST OF YOUR LIFE
Thursday, Aug. 19		
Friday, Aug. 20		

Saturday, Aug. 21	Sunday, Aug. 22 ○ *Full Moon*

THE ORIGINAL STUDENT CALENDAR

AUGUST 2021						
S	M	T	W	T	F	S
1	**2**	3	4	5	6	7
8	9	10	11	12	13	14
15	16	17	18	19	20	21
22	**23**	**24**	**25**	**26**	**27**	**28**
29	30	31				

TO DO THIS WEEK

APPOINTMENTS & ASSIGNMENTS	GENERAL STUDY	THE REST OF YOUR LIFE
Monday, Aug. 23		
Tuesday, Aug. 24		
Wednesday, Aug. 25		

THE ORIGINAL STUDENT CALENDAR

TO DO THIS MONTH	Whatever you do, always give 100%. Unless you're donating blood. — *Bill Murray*

APPOINTMENTS & ASSIGNMENTS	GENERAL STUDY	THE REST OF YOUR LIFE
Thursday, Aug. 26		
Friday, Aug. 27		

Saturday, Aug. 28	Sunday, Aug. 29

THE ORIGINAL STUDENT CALENDAR

SEPTEMBER 2021

S	M	T	W	T	F	S
	30	31	**1**	**2**	**3**	**4**
5	**6**	7	8	9	10	11
12	13	14	15	16	17	18
19	20	21	22	23	24	25
26	27	28	29	30		

TO DO THIS WEEK

APPOINTMENTS & ASSIGNMENTS	GENERAL STUDY	THE REST OF YOUR LIFE
Monday, Aug. 30		
Tuesday, Aug. 31		
Wednesday, Sept. 1		

THE ORIGINAL STUDENT CALENDAR

TO DO THIS MONTH	I have learned over the years that when one's mind is made up, this diminishes fear. — *Rosa Parks*

APPOINTMENTS & ASSIGNMENTS	GENERAL STUDY	THE REST OF YOUR LIFE
Thursday, Sept. 2		
Friday, Sept. 3		

Saturday, Sept. 4	Sunday, Sept. 5

THE ORIGINAL STUDENT CALENDAR

SEPTEMBER 2021

S	M	T	W	T	F	S
			1	2	3	4
5	**6**	**7**	**8**	**9**	**10**	**11**
12	13	14	15	16	17	18
19	20	21	22	23	24	25
26	27	28	29	30		

TO DO THIS WEEK

APPOINTMENTS & ASSIGNMENTS | **GENERAL STUDY** | **THE REST OF YOUR LIFE**

Monday, Sept. 6 *Labour Day, ● New Moon*

Tuesday, Sept. 7 *First day of Rosh Hashanah*

Wednesday, Sept. 8

THE ORIGINAL STUDENT CALENDAR

TO DO THIS MONTH	
	A hunch is creativity trying to tell you something. — *Frank Capra*

APPOINTMENTS & ASSIGNMENTS	GENERAL STUDY	THE REST OF YOUR LIFE
Thursday, Sept. 9		
Friday, Sept. 10		

Saturday, Sept. 11	Sunday, Sept. 12

THE ORIGINAL STUDENT CALENDAR

SEPTEMBER 2021						
S	M	T	W	T	F	S
			1	2	3	4
5	**6**	7	8	9	10	11
12	**13**	**14**	**15**	**16**	**17**	**18**
19	20	21	22	23	24	25
26	27	28	29	30		

TO DO THIS WEEK

APPOINTMENTS & ASSIGNMENTS	GENERAL STUDY	THE REST OF YOUR LIFE
Monday, Sept. 13		
Tuesday, Sept. 14		
Wednesday, Sept. 15		

THE ORIGINAL STUDENT CALENDAR

TO DO THIS MONTH	In a perfect dream, things would be set exactly the way you would want them. But I think it's more interesting that in real life, things aren't exactly the way you planned. — *Naomi Osaka*

APPOINTMENTS & ASSIGNMENTS	GENERAL STUDY	THE REST OF YOUR LIFE
Thursday, Sept. 16 *Yom Kippur*		
Friday, Sept. 17		

Saturday, Sept. 18	Sunday, Sept. 19

THE ORIGINAL STUDENT CALENDAR

SEPTEMBER 2021

S	M	T	W	T	F	S
			1	2	3	4
5	**6**	7	8	9	10	11
12	13	14	15	16	17	18
19	**20**	**21**	**22**	**23**	**24**	**25**
26	27	28	29	30		

TO DO THIS WEEK

APPOINTMENTS & ASSIGNMENTS | **GENERAL STUDY** | **THE REST OF YOUR LIFE**

Monday, Sept. 20 ○ *Full Moon*

Tuesday, Sept. 21 *U.N. International Day of Peace*

Wednesday, Sept. 22 *Autumnal Equinox*

THE ORIGINAL STUDENT CALENDAR

TO DO THIS MONTH

> We can all, always, let someone, somewhere, know they are not alone.
>
> — *Sara Genn*

APPOINTMENTS & ASSIGNMENTS	**GENERAL STUDY**	**THE REST OF YOUR LIFE**
Thursday, Sept. 23		
Friday, Sept. 24		

Saturday, Sept. 25	Sunday, Sept. 26

THE ORIGINAL STUDENT CALENDAR

OCTOBER 2021							TO DO THIS WEEK
S	M	T	W	T	F	S	
	27	28	29	30	**1**	**2**	
3	4	5	6	7	8	9	
10	**11**	12	13	14	15	16	
17	18	19	20	21	22	23	
24	25	26	27	28	29	30	
31							

APPOINTMENTS & ASSIGNMENTS	GENERAL STUDY	THE REST OF YOUR LIFE
Monday, Sept. 27		
Tuesday, Sept. 28		
Wednesday, Sept. 29		

THE ORIGINAL STUDENT CALENDAR

TO DO THIS MONTH

When you don't have much time, a routine helps make the little time you have count. When you have all the time in the world, a routine helps you make sure you don't waste it.

— *Austin Kleon*

APPOINTMENTS & ASSIGNMENTS	GENERAL STUDY	THE REST OF YOUR LIFE
Thursday, Sept. 30		
Friday, Oct. 1		

Saturday, Oct. 2	Sunday, Oct. 3

THE ORIGINAL STUDENT CALENDAR

OCTOBER 2021

S	M	T	W	T	F	S
					1	2
3	**4**	**5**	**6**	**7**	**8**	**9**
10	**11**	12	13	14	15	16
17	18	19	20	21	22	23
24	25	26	27	28	29	30
31						

TO DO THIS WEEK

APPOINTMENTS & ASSIGNMENTS	GENERAL STUDY	THE REST OF YOUR LIFE
Monday, Oct. 4		
Tuesday, Oct. 5		
Wednesday, Oct. 6 ● *New Moon*		

THE ORIGINAL STUDENT CALENDAR

TO DO THIS MONTH

Fairy tales are more than true – not because they tell us dragons exist, but because they tell us dragons can be beaten.

— *G.K. Chesterton*

APPOINTMENTS & ASSIGNMENTS	GENERAL STUDY	THE REST OF YOUR LIFE
Thursday, Oct. 7		
Friday, Oct. 8		

Saturday, Oct. 9	Sunday, Oct. 10

THE ORIGINAL STUDENT CALENDAR

OCTOBER 2021						
S	**M**	**T**	**W**	**T**	**F**	**S**
					1	2
3	4	5	6	7	8	9
10	**11**	**12**	**13**	**14**	**15**	**16**
17	18	19	20	21	22	23
24	25	26	27	28	29	30
31						

TO DO THIS WEEK

APPOINTMENTS & ASSIGNMENTS	GENERAL STUDY	THE REST OF YOUR LIFE
Monday, Oct. 11 *Thanksgiving Day (Canada), Columbus Day (U.S.)*		
Tuesday, Oct. 12		
Wednesday, Oct. 13		

THE ORIGINAL STUDENT CALENDAR

TO DO THIS MONTH	
	I'm so glad I live in a world where there are Octobers. — *L.M. Montgomery*

APPOINTMENTS & ASSIGNMENTS	GENERAL STUDY	THE REST OF YOUR LIFE
Thursday, Oct. 14		
Friday, Oct. 15		

Saturday, Oct. 16	Sunday, Oct. 17

THE ORIGINAL STUDENT CALENDAR

OCTOBER 2021

S	M	T	W	T	F	S
					1	2
3	4	5	6	7	8	9
10	**11**	12	13	14	15	16
17	**18**	**19**	**20**	**21**	**22**	**23**
24	25	26	27	28	29	30
31						

TO DO THIS WEEK

APPOINTMENTS & ASSIGNMENTS	GENERAL STUDY	THE REST OF YOUR LIFE
Monday, Oct. 18		
Tuesday, Oct. 19		
Wednesday, Oct. 20 ○ *Full Moon*		

THE ORIGINAL STUDENT CALENDAR

TO DO THIS MONTH

If you put yourself in an environment with lots of different perspectives, you yourself are going to have better, sharper, more original ideas.

— *Steven Johnson*

APPOINTMENTS & ASSIGNMENTS	GENERAL STUDY	THE REST OF YOUR LIFE
Thursday, Oct. 21		
Friday, Oct. 22		

Saturday, Oct. 23	Sunday, Oct. 24

THE ORIGINAL STUDENT CALENDAR

OCTOBER 2021

S	M	T	W	T	F	S
					1	2
3	4	5	6	7	8	9
10	**11**	12	13	14	15	16
17	18	19	20	21	22	23
24	**25**	**26**	**27**	**28**	**29**	**30**
31						

TO DO THIS WEEK

APPOINTMENTS & ASSIGNMENTS	GENERAL STUDY	THE REST OF YOUR LIFE
Monday, Oct. 25		
Tuesday, Oct. 26		
Wednesday, Oct. 27		

THE ORIGINAL STUDENT CALENDAR

TO DO THIS MONTH	
	Dance first. Think later. It's the natural order. — *Samuel Beckett*

APPOINTMENTS & ASSIGNMENTS	GENERAL STUDY	THE REST OF YOUR LIFE
Thursday, Oct. 28		
Friday, Oct. 29		

Saturday, Oct. 30	Sunday, Oct. 31 *Halloween*

THE ORIGINAL STUDENT CALENDAR

NOVEMBER 2021

S	M	T	W	T	F	S
	1	**2**	**3**	**4**	**5**	**6**
7	8	9	10	**11**	12	13
14	15	16	17	18	19	20
21	22	23	24	**25**	26	27
28	29	30				

TO DO THIS WEEK

APPOINTMENTS & ASSIGNMENTS	GENERAL STUDY	THE REST OF YOUR LIFE
Monday, Nov. 1		
Tuesday, Nov. 2		
Wednesday, Nov. 3		

THE ORIGINAL STUDENT CALENDAR

TO DO THIS MONTH

Read something that upsets your worldview, that makes you feel a little bit uncomfortable.

— *Esi Edugyan*

APPOINTMENTS & ASSIGNMENTS	GENERAL STUDY	THE REST OF YOUR LIFE
Thursday, Nov. 4 *Diwali,* ● *New Moon*		
Friday, Nov. 5		

Saturday, Nov. 6	Sunday, Nov. 7 *Daylight Saving Time ends (set clock back one hour)*

THE ORIGINAL STUDENT CALENDAR

NOVEMBER 2021						
S	M	T	W	T	F	S
	1	2	3	4	5	6
7	**8**	**9**	**10**	**11**	**12**	**13**
14	15	16	17	18	19	20
21	22	23	24	**25**	26	27
28	29	30				

TO DO THIS WEEK

APPOINTMENTS & ASSIGNMENTS	GENERAL STUDY	THE REST OF YOUR LIFE
Monday, Nov. 8		
Tuesday, Nov. 9		
Wednesday, Nov. 10		

THE ORIGINAL STUDENT CALENDAR

TO DO THIS MONTH

I think that cynicism can often be mistaken for wisdom.

— *Sarah Polley*

APPOINTMENTS & ASSIGNMENTS | **GENERAL STUDY** | **THE REST OF YOUR LIFE**

Thursday, Nov. 11 *Remembrance Day (Canada), Veterans' Day (U.S.)*

Friday, Nov. 12

Saturday, Nov. 13

Sunday, Nov. 14

THE ORIGINAL STUDENT CALENDAR

NOVEMBER 2021						
S	**M**	**T**	**W**	**T**	**F**	**S**
	1	2	3	4	5	6
7	8	9	10	**11**	12	13
14	**15**	**16**	**17**	**18**	**19**	**20**
21	22	23	24	**25**	26	27
28	29	30				

TO DO THIS WEEK

APPOINTMENTS & ASSIGNMENTS	GENERAL STUDY	THE REST OF YOUR LIFE
Monday, Nov. 15		
Tuesday, Nov. 16		
Wednesday, Nov. 17		

THE ORIGINAL STUDENT CALENDAR

TO DO THIS MONTH

I don't think one can explain growth. It is silent and subtle. One does not keep digging up a plant to see how it grows.

— *Emily Carr*

APPOINTMENTS & ASSIGNMENTS	GENERAL STUDY	THE REST OF YOUR LIFE
Thursday, Nov. 18		
Friday, Nov. 19 ○ *Full Moon*		

Saturday, Nov. 20
Universal Children's Day

Sunday, Nov. 21

THE ORIGINAL STUDENT CALENDAR

NOVEMBER 2021						
S	M	T	W	T	F	S
	1	2	3	4	5	6
7	8	9	10	**11**	12	13
14	15	16	17	18	19	20
21	**22**	**23**	**24**	**25**	**26**	**27**
28	29	30				

TO DO THIS WEEK

APPOINTMENTS & ASSIGNMENTS	GENERAL STUDY	THE REST OF YOUR LIFE
Monday, Nov. 22		
Tuesday, Nov. 23		
Wednesday, Nov. 24		

THE ORIGINAL STUDENT CALENDAR

TO DO THIS MONTH	All the world is birthday cake, so take a piece, but not too much. — *George Harrison*

APPOINTMENTS & ASSIGNMENTS	GENERAL STUDY	THE REST OF YOUR LIFE
Thursday, Nov. 25 *Thanksgiving Day (U.S.)*		
Friday, Nov. 26		

Saturday, Nov. 27	Sunday, Nov. 28

THE ORIGINAL STUDENT CALENDAR

DECEMBER 2021

S	M	T	W	T	F	S
	29	30	**1**	**2**	**3**	**4**
5	6	7	8	9	10	11
12	13	14	15	16	17	18
19	20	21	22	23	24	**25**
26	27	28	29	30	31	

TO DO THIS WEEK

APPOINTMENTS & ASSIGNMENTS | **GENERAL STUDY** | **THE REST OF YOUR LIFE**

Monday, Nov. 29 *First day of Hanukkah*

Tuesday, Nov. 30

Wednesday, Dec. 1

THE ORIGINAL STUDENT CALENDAR

TO DO THIS MONTH

As long as you can start,
you are all right.
The juice will come.

— *Ernest Hemingway*

APPOINTMENTS & ASSIGNMENTS	GENERAL STUDY	THE REST OF YOUR LIFE
Thursday, Dec. 2		
Friday, Dec. 3 ● *New Moon*		

Saturday, Dec. 4	Sunday, Dec. 5

THE ORIGINAL STUDENT CALENDAR

DECEMBER 2021

S	M	T	W	T	F	S
			1	2	3	4
5	**6**	**7**	**8**	**9**	**10**	**11**
12	13	14	15	16	17	18
19	20	21	22	23	24	**25**
26	27	28	29	30	31	

TO DO THIS WEEK

APPOINTMENTS & ASSIGNMENTS	GENERAL STUDY	THE REST OF YOUR LIFE
Monday, Dec. 6		
Tuesday, Dec. 7		
Wednesday, Dec. 8		

THE ORIGINAL STUDENT CALENDAR

TO DO THIS MONTH

> The way to do research is to attack the facts at the point of greatest astonishment.
>
> — *Celia Green*

APPOINTMENTS & ASSIGNMENTS	GENERAL STUDY	THE REST OF YOUR LIFE
Thursday, Dec. 9		
Friday, Dec. 10		

Saturday, Dec. 11	Sunday, Dec. 12

THE ORIGINAL STUDENT CALENDAR

DECEMBER 2021

S	M	T	W	T	F	S
			1	2	3	4
5	6	7	8	9	10	11
12	**13**	**14**	**15**	**16**	**17**	**18**
19	20	21	22	23	24	**25**
26	27	28	29	30	31	

TO DO THIS WEEK

APPOINTMENTS & ASSIGNMENTS	GENERAL STUDY	THE REST OF YOUR LIFE
Monday, Dec. 13		
Tuesday, Dec. 14		
Wednesday, Dec. 15		

THE ORIGINAL STUDENT CALENDAR

TO DO THIS MONTH	
	If you're overwhelmed by the whole, break it down into pieces. — *Chuck Close*

APPOINTMENTS & ASSIGNMENTS	GENERAL STUDY	THE REST OF YOUR LIFE
Thursday, Dec. 16		
Friday, Dec. 17		

Saturday, Dec. 18 ○ *Full Moon*	Sunday, Dec. 19

THE ORIGINAL STUDENT CALENDAR

DECEMBER 2021						
S	M	T	W	T	F	S
			1	2	3	4
5	6	7	8	9	10	11
12	13	14	15	16	17	18
19	**20**	**21**	**22**	**23**	**24**	**25**
26	27	28	29	30	31	

TO DO THIS WEEK

APPOINTMENTS & ASSIGNMENTS	GENERAL STUDY	THE REST OF YOUR LIFE
Monday, Dec. 20		
Tuesday, Dec. 21 *Winter Solstice*		
Wednesday, Dec. 22		

THE ORIGINAL STUDENT CALENDAR

TO DO THIS MONTH

If we can look up and acknowledge each other, we can help each other more than we'll ever know.

— *Clara Hughes*

APPOINTMENTS & ASSIGNMENTS	GENERAL STUDY	THE REST OF YOUR LIFE
Thursday, Dec. 23		
Friday, Dec. 24		

Saturday, Dec. 25 *Christmas Day*	Sunday, Dec. 26 *Boxing Day (Canada)*

THE ORIGINAL STUDENT CALENDAR

DECEMBER 2021						
S	M	T	W	T	F	S
			1	2	3	4
5	6	7	8	9	10	11
12	13	14	15	16	17	18
19	20	21	22	23	24	**25**
26	**27**	**28**	**29**	**30**	**31**	1
2						

TO DO THIS WEEK

APPOINTMENTS & ASSIGNMENTS	GENERAL STUDY	THE REST OF YOUR LIFE
Monday, Dec. 27		
Tuesday, Dec. 28		
Wednesday, Dec. 29		

THE ORIGINAL STUDENT CALENDAR

TO DO THIS MONTH

Let us make our future now, and let us make our dreams tomorrow's reality.

— *Malala Yousafzai*

APPOINTMENTS & ASSIGNMENTS	GENERAL STUDY	THE REST OF YOUR LIFE
Thursday, Dec. 30		
Friday, Dec. 31 *New Year's Eve*		

Saturday, Jan. 1 *New Year's Day*	Sunday, Jan. 2 ● *New Moon*

THE ORIGINAL STUDENT CALENDAR

JANUARY 2022

S	M	T	W	T	F	S
						1
2	**3**	**4**	**5**	**6**	**7**	**8**
9	10	11	12	13	14	15
16	17	18	19	20	21	22
23	24	25	26	27	28	29
30	31					

TO DO THIS WEEK

APPOINTMENTS & ASSIGNMENTS	GENERAL STUDY	THE REST OF YOUR LIFE
Monday, Jan. 3		
Tuesday, Jan. 4		
Wednesday, Jan. 5		

THE ORIGINAL STUDENT CALENDAR

TO DO THIS MONTH	Rarely are opportunities presented to you in a perfect way. In a nice little box with a yellow bow on top. Opportunities — the good ones — are messy, confusing, and hard to recognize. They're risky. They challenge you. — *Susan Wojcicki*

APPOINTMENTS & ASSIGNMENTS	GENERAL STUDY	THE REST OF YOUR LIFE
Thursday, Jan. 6		
Friday, Jan. 7		

Saturday, Jan. 8	Sunday, Jan. 9

THE ORIGINAL STUDENT CALENDAR

JANUARY 2022						
S	M	T	W	T	F	S
						1
2	3	4	5	6	7	8
9	**10**	**11**	**12**	**13**	**14**	**15**
16	17	18	19	20	21	22
23	24	25	26	27	28	29
30	31					

TO DO THIS WEEK

APPOINTMENTS & ASSIGNMENTS	GENERAL STUDY	THE REST OF YOUR LIFE
Monday, Jan. 10		
Tuesday, Jan. 11		
Wednesday, Jan. 12		

THE ORIGINAL STUDENT CALENDAR

TO DO THIS MONTH	
	Sometimes a little comfort food can go a long way. — *Benjamin Bratt*

APPOINTMENTS & ASSIGNMENTS	GENERAL STUDY	THE REST OF YOUR LIFE
Thursday, Jan. 13		
Friday, Jan. 14		

Saturday, Jan. 15	Sunday, Jan. 16

THE ORIGINAL STUDENT CALENDAR

JANUARY 2022						
S	**M**	**T**	**W**	**T**	**F**	**S**
						1
2	3	4	5	6	7	8
9	10	11	12	13	14	15
16	**17**	**18**	**19**	**20**	**21**	**22**
23	24	25	26	27	28	29
30	31					

TO DO THIS WEEK

APPOINTMENTS & ASSIGNMENTS **GENERAL STUDY** **THE REST OF YOUR LIFE**

Monday, Jan. 17 *Martin Luther King, Jr. Day (U.S.),* ○ *Full Moon*

Tuesday, Jan. 18

Wednesday, Jan. 19

THE ORIGINAL STUDENT CALENDAR

TO DO THIS MONTH	
	Of course you could despair. You can walk down the street of any city, any afternoon, and look around you, but what you've got to remember — everyone you're looking at is also you. — *James Baldwin*

APPOINTMENTS & ASSIGNMENTS	GENERAL STUDY	THE REST OF YOUR LIFE
Thursday, Jan. 20		
Friday, Jan. 21		

Saturday, Jan. 22	Sunday, Jan. 23

THE ORIGINAL STUDENT CALENDAR

JANUARY 2022						
S	**M**	**T**	**W**	**T**	**F**	**S**
						1
2	3	4	5	6	7	8
9	10	11	12	13	14	15
16	17	18	19	20	21	22
23	**24**	**25**	**26**	**27**	**28**	**29**
30	31					

TO DO THIS WEEK

APPOINTMENTS & ASSIGNMENTS	GENERAL STUDY	THE REST OF YOUR LIFE
Monday, Jan. 24		
Tuesday, Jan. 25		
Wednesday, Jan. 26		

THE ORIGINAL STUDENT CALENDAR

TO DO THIS MONTH

Flow is an optimal state in which you feel totally engaged in an activity — you're neither bored nor anxious, and you don't question your own adequacy. Hours pass without your noticing.

— *Susan Cain*

APPOINTMENTS & ASSIGNMENTS	GENERAL STUDY	THE REST OF YOUR LIFE
Thursday, Jan. 27		
Friday, Jan. 28		

Saturday, Jan. 29	Sunday, Jan. 30

THE ORIGINAL STUDENT CALENDAR

FEBRUARY 2022

S	M	T	W	T	F	S
		1	**2**	**3**	**4**	**5**
6	7	8	9	10	11	12
13	14	15	16	17	18	19
20	**21**	22	23	24	25	26
27	28					

TO DO THIS WEEK

APPOINTMENTS & ASSIGNMENTS | **GENERAL STUDY** | **THE REST OF YOUR LIFE**

Monday, Jan. 31 ● *New Moon*

Tuesday, Feb. 1 *Chinese New Year (Year of the Tiger)*

Wednesday, Feb. 2 *Groundhog Day*

THE ORIGINAL STUDENT CALENDAR

TO DO THIS MONTH	
	Every writer I admire is my teacher. — *Sandra Cisneros*

APPOINTMENTS & ASSIGNMENTS	GENERAL STUDY	THE REST OF YOUR LIFE
Thursday, Feb. 3		
Friday, Feb. 4		

Saturday, Feb. 5	Sunday, Feb. 6

THE ORIGINAL STUDENT CALENDAR

FEBRUARY 2022

S	M	T	W	T	F	S
		1	2	3	4	5
6	**7**	**8**	**9**	**10**	**11**	**12**
13	14	15	16	17	18	19
20	**21**	22	23	24	25	26
27	28					

TO DO THIS WEEK

APPOINTMENTS & ASSIGNMENTS	GENERAL STUDY	THE REST OF YOUR LIFE
Monday, Feb. 7		
Tuesday, Feb. 8		
Wednesday, Feb. 9		

THE ORIGINAL STUDENT CALENDAR

TO DO THIS MONTH	When something comes into my mind, I like to follow it. — *Zadie Smith*

APPOINTMENTS & ASSIGNMENTS	GENERAL STUDY	THE REST OF YOUR LIFE
Thursday, Feb. 10		
Friday, Feb. 11		

Saturday, Feb. 12	Sunday, Feb. 13

THE ORIGINAL STUDENT CALENDAR

FEBRUARY 2022

S	M	T	W	T	F	S
		1	2	3	4	5
6	7	8	9	10	11	12
13	**14**	**15**	**16**	**17**	**18**	**19**
20	**21**	22	23	24	25	26
27	28					

TO DO THIS WEEK

APPOINTMENTS & ASSIGNMENTS **GENERAL STUDY** **THE REST OF YOUR LIFE**

Monday, Feb. 14 *Valentine's Day*

Tuesday, Feb. 15

Wednesday, Feb. 16 ○ *Full Moon*

THE ORIGINAL STUDENT CALENDAR

TO DO THIS MONTH

You are so much sunshine in every square inch.

— *Walt Whitman*

APPOINTMENTS & ASSIGNMENTS	GENERAL STUDY	THE REST OF YOUR LIFE
Thursday, Feb. 17		
Friday, Feb. 18		

Saturday, Feb. 19	Sunday, Feb. 20

THE ORIGINAL STUDENT CALENDAR

FEBRUARY 2022						
S	M	T	W	T	F	S
		1	2	3	4	5
6	7	8	9	10	11	12
13	14	15	16	17	18	19
20	**21**	**22**	**23**	**24**	**25**	**26**
27	28					

TO DO THIS WEEK

APPOINTMENTS & ASSIGNMENTS	GENERAL STUDY	THE REST OF YOUR LIFE
Monday, Feb. 21 *Family/Heritage Day (Canada), Presidents' Day (U.S.)*		
Tuesday, Feb. 22		
Wednesday, Feb. 23		

THE ORIGINAL STUDENT CALENDAR

TO DO THIS MONTH	Any time you talk to anyone about something that they love, they're, like, their most beautiful. It's a cool gift to get to talk to people about what they love. — *Amy Poehler*

APPOINTMENTS & ASSIGNMENTS	GENERAL STUDY	THE REST OF YOUR LIFE
Thursday, Feb. 24		
Friday, Feb. 25		

Saturday, Feb. 26	Sunday, Feb. 27

THE ORIGINAL STUDENT CALENDAR

MARCH 2022						
S	M	T	W	T	F	S
	28	**1**	**2**	**3**	**4**	**5**
6	7	8	9	10	11	12
13	14	15	16	17	18	19
20	21	22	23	24	25	26
27	28	29	30	31		

TO DO THIS WEEK

APPOINTMENTS & ASSIGNMENTS	GENERAL STUDY	THE REST OF YOUR LIFE
Monday, Feb. 28		
Tuesday, Mar. 1		
Wednesday, Mar. 2 *Ash Wednesday, ● New Moon*		

THE ORIGINAL STUDENT CALENDAR

TO DO THIS MONTH

Why does getting ahead always have to involve getting up early?

— *Elizabeth Jane Howard*

APPOINTMENTS & ASSIGNMENTS	GENERAL STUDY	THE REST OF YOUR LIFE
Thursday, Mar. 3		
Friday, Mar. 4		

Saturday, Mar. 5	Sunday, Mar. 6

THE ORIGINAL STUDENT CALENDAR

MARCH 2022						
S	M	T	W	T	F	S
		1	2	3	4	5
6	**7**	**8**	**9**	**10**	**11**	**12**
13	14	15	16	17	18	19
20	21	22	23	24	25	26
27	28	29	30	31		

TO DO THIS WEEK

APPOINTMENTS & ASSIGNMENTS	GENERAL STUDY	THE REST OF YOUR LIFE
Monday, Mar. 7		
Tuesday, Mar. 8 *International Women's Day*		
Wednesday, Mar. 9		

THE ORIGINAL STUDENT CALENDAR

TO DO THIS MONTH

We have a voice and a choice in the kind of future we have.

—Joy Buolamwini

APPOINTMENTS & ASSIGNMENTS	GENERAL STUDY	THE REST OF YOUR LIFE
Thursday, Mar. 10		
Friday, Mar. 11		

Saturday, Mar. 12	Sunday, Mar. 13 *Daylight Saving Time begins (set clock ahead one hour)*

THE ORIGINAL STUDENT CALENDAR

MARCH 2022

S	M	T	W	T	F	S
		1	2	3	4	5
6	7	8	9	10	11	12
13	**14**	**15**	**16**	**17**	**18**	**19**
20	21	22	23	24	25	26
27	28	29	30	31		

TO DO THIS WEEK

APPOINTMENTS & ASSIGNMENTS	GENERAL STUDY	THE REST OF YOUR LIFE
Monday, Mar. 14		
Tuesday, Mar. 15		
Wednesday, Mar. 16		

THE ORIGINAL STUDENT CALENDAR

TO DO THIS MONTH

Relaxing is not solely a physical thing for the body. Your brain needs to chill out, too.

— *Dr. Sanjay Gupta*

APPOINTMENTS & ASSIGNMENTS **GENERAL STUDY** **THE REST OF YOUR LIFE**

Thursday, Mar. 17 *Purim, St. Patrick's Day*

Friday, Mar. 18 ○ *Full Moon*

Saturday, Mar. 19 *Holi*

Sunday, Mar. 20 *Vernal Equinox*

THE ORIGINAL STUDENT CALENDAR

MARCH 2022

S	M	T	W	T	F	S
		1	2	3	4	5
6	7	8	9	10	11	12
13	14	15	16	17	18	19
20	**21**	**22**	**23**	**24**	**25**	**26**
27	28	29	30	31		

TO DO THIS WEEK

APPOINTMENTS & ASSIGNMENTS	GENERAL STUDY	THE REST OF YOUR LIFE
Monday, Mar. 21		
Tuesday, Mar. 22		
Wednesday, Mar. 23		

THE ORIGINAL STUDENT CALENDAR

TO DO THIS MONTH	
	Finishing a good book is like leaving a good friend. — *William Feather*

APPOINTMENTS & ASSIGNMENTS	GENERAL STUDY	THE REST OF YOUR LIFE
Thursday, Mar. 24		
Friday, Mar. 25		

Saturday, Mar. 26	Sunday, Mar. 27

THE ORIGINAL STUDENT CALENDAR

APRIL 2022						
S	M	T	W	T	F	S
	28	29	30	31	**1**	**2**
3	4	5	6	7	8	9
10	11	12	13	14	**15**	16
17	18	19	20	21	22	23
24	25	26	27	28	29	30

TO DO THIS WEEK

APPOINTMENTS & ASSIGNMENTS	GENERAL STUDY	THE REST OF YOUR LIFE
Monday, Mar. 28		
Tuesday, Mar. 29		
Wednesday, Mar. 30		

THE ORIGINAL STUDENT CALENDAR

TO DO THIS MONTH

Don't draw invisible boundaries for yourself everywhere. Don't create a set of beliefs about yourself that are going to box you in.

— *Breena Clarke*

APPOINTMENTS & ASSIGNMENTS	GENERAL STUDY	THE REST OF YOUR LIFE
Thursday, Mar. 31		
Friday, Apr. 1 ● *New Moon*		

Saturday, Apr. 2

Sunday, Apr. 3
First day of Ramadan

THE ORIGINAL STUDENT CALENDAR

APRIL 2022						
S	M	T	W	T	F	S
					1	2
3	**4**	**5**	**6**	**7**	**8**	**9**
10	11	12	13	14	**15**	16
17	18	19	20	21	22	23
24	25	26	27	28	29	30

TO DO THIS WEEK

APPOINTMENTS & ASSIGNMENTS	GENERAL STUDY	THE REST OF YOUR LIFE
Monday, Apr. 4		
Tuesday, Apr. 5		
Wednesday, Apr. 6		

THE ORIGINAL STUDENT CALENDAR

TO DO THIS MONTH	
	Spring is a wondrous necessity. — *Vera Cleaver*

APPOINTMENTS & ASSIGNMENTS	GENERAL STUDY	THE REST OF YOUR LIFE
Thursday, Apr. 7		
Friday, Apr. 8		

Saturday, Apr. 9	Sunday, Apr. 10 *Palm Sunday*

THE ORIGINAL STUDENT CALENDAR

APRIL 2022

S	M	T	W	T	F	S
					1	2
3	4	5	6	7	8	9
10	**11**	**12**	**13**	**14**	**15**	**16**
17	18	19	20	21	22	23
24	25	26	27	28	29	30

TO DO THIS WEEK

APPOINTMENTS & ASSIGNMENTS	GENERAL STUDY	THE REST OF YOUR LIFE
Monday, Apr. 11		
Tuesday, Apr. 12		
Wednesday, Apr. 13		

THE ORIGINAL STUDENT CALENDAR

TO DO THIS MONTH

There can be no greater gift than that of giving one's time and energy to help others without expecting anything in return.

— *Nelson Mandela*

APPOINTMENTS & ASSIGNMENTS	GENERAL STUDY	THE REST OF YOUR LIFE
Thursday, Apr. 14		
Friday, Apr. 15 *Good Friday*		

Saturday, Apr. 16 *First Day of Passover, ○ Full Moon*	Sunday, Apr. 17 *Easter*

THE ORIGINAL STUDENT CALENDAR

APRIL 2022

S	M	T	W	T	F	S
					1	2
3	4	5	6	7	8	9
10	11	12	13	14	**15**	16
17	**18**	**19**	**20**	**21**	**22**	**23**
24	25	26	27	28	29	30

TO DO THIS WEEK

APPOINTMENTS & ASSIGNMENTS	GENERAL STUDY	THE REST OF YOUR LIFE
Monday, Apr. 18		
Tuesday, Apr. 19		
Wednesday, Apr. 20		

THE ORIGINAL STUDENT CALENDAR

TO DO THIS MONTH

You don't need to be a politician
to make it your mission
to conserve, to protect, to preserve
that one and only home
that is ours.

— *Amanda Gorman*

APPOINTMENTS & ASSIGNMENTS	GENERAL STUDY	THE REST OF YOUR LIFE
Thursday, Apr. 21		
Friday, Apr. 22 *Earth Day*		

Saturday, Apr. 23	Sunday, Apr. 24

THE ORIGINAL STUDENT CALENDAR

APRIL 2022

S	M	T	W	T	F	S
					1	2
3	4	5	6	7	8	9
10	11	12	13	14	**15**	16
17	18	19	20	21	22	23
24	**25**	**26**	**27**	**28**	**29**	**30**
1						

TO DO THIS WEEK

APPOINTMENTS & ASSIGNMENTS	GENERAL STUDY	THE REST OF YOUR LIFE
Monday, Apr. 25		
Tuesday, Apr. 26		
Wednesday, Apr. 27		

THE ORIGINAL STUDENT CALENDAR

TO DO THIS MONTH

A rainy day is
the perfect time for
a walk in the woods.

— *Rachel Carson*

APPOINTMENTS & ASSIGNMENTS	GENERAL STUDY	THE REST OF YOUR LIFE
Thursday, Apr. 28		
Friday, Apr. 29		

Saturday, Apr. 30 ● *New Moon*	Sunday, May 1

THE ORIGINAL STUDENT CALENDAR

MAY 2022

S	M	T	W	T	F	S
1	**2**	**3**	**4**	**5**	**6**	**7**
8	9	10	11	12	13	14
15	16	17	18	19	20	21
22	**23**	24	25	26	27	28
29	**30**	31				

TO DO THIS WEEK

APPOINTMENTS & ASSIGNMENTS	GENERAL STUDY	THE REST OF YOUR LIFE
Monday, May 2		
Tuesday, May 3		
Wednesday, May 4		

THE ORIGINAL STUDENT CALENDAR

TO DO THIS MONTH

Be not too critical of others, and love much.

— *Julia Huxley, to her son Aldous*

APPOINTMENTS & ASSIGNMENTS	GENERAL STUDY	THE REST OF YOUR LIFE
Thursday, May 5		
Friday, May 6		

Saturday, May 7	Sunday, May 8 *Mother's Day (Canada, U.S.)*

THE ORIGINAL STUDENT CALENDAR

MAY 2022

S	M	T	W	T	F	S
1	2	3	4	5	6	7
8	**9**	**10**	**11**	**12**	**13**	**14**
15	16	17	18	19	20	21
22	**23**	24	25	26	27	28
29	**30**	31				

TO DO THIS WEEK

APPOINTMENTS & ASSIGNMENTS	GENERAL STUDY	THE REST OF YOUR LIFE
Monday, May 9		
Tuesday, May 10		
Wednesday, May 11		

THE ORIGINAL STUDENT CALENDAR

TO DO THIS MONTH

Sometimes you have to wander a bit, and do what you don't want to in order to figure out what it is you're supposed to do.

— *Larry David*

APPOINTMENTS & ASSIGNMENTS	GENERAL STUDY	THE REST OF YOUR LIFE
Thursday, May 12		
Friday, May 13		

Saturday, May 14	Sunday, May 15 ○ *Full Moon*

THE ORIGINAL STUDENT CALENDAR

MAY 2022						
S	M	T	W	T	F	S
1	2	3	4	5	6	7
8	9	10	11	12	13	14
15	**16**	**17**	**18**	**19**	**20**	**21**
22	**23**	24	25	26	27	28
29	**30**	31				

TO DO THIS WEEK

APPOINTMENTS & ASSIGNMENTS	GENERAL STUDY	THE REST OF YOUR LIFE
Monday, May 16		
Tuesday, May 17		
Wednesday, May 18		

THE ORIGINAL STUDENT CALENDAR

TO DO THIS MONTH

The tall birch trees glitter in the afternoon light as their many leaves rattle, sounding like a gentle rain stick. Listening, I connect to the world around me.

—*Julia Cameron*

APPOINTMENTS & ASSIGNMENTS	GENERAL STUDY	THE REST OF YOUR LIFE
Thursday, May 19		
Friday, May 20		

Saturday, May 21	Sunday, May 22

THE ORIGINAL STUDENT CALENDAR

MAY 2022

S	M	T	W	T	F	S
1	2	3	4	5	6	7
8	9	10	11	12	13	14
15	16	17	18	19	20	21
22	**23**	**24**	**25**	**26**	**27**	**28**
29	**30**	31				

TO DO THIS WEEK

APPOINTMENTS & ASSIGNMENTS	GENERAL STUDY	THE REST OF YOUR LIFE
Monday, May 23 *Victoria Day (Canada)*		
Tuesday, May 24		
Wednesday, May 25		

THE ORIGINAL STUDENT CALENDAR

TO DO THIS MONTH

We constantly feel like we need to improve ourselves, but in fact, we're already pretty great. We just need to see that.

— *Leo Babauta*

APPOINTMENTS & ASSIGNMENTS	GENERAL STUDY	THE REST OF YOUR LIFE
Thursday, May 26		
Friday, May 27		

Saturday, May 28	Sunday, May 29

THE ORIGINAL STUDENT CALENDAR

JUNE 2022

S	M	T	W	T	F	S
	30	31	**1**	**2**	**3**	**4**
5	6	7	8	9	10	11
12	13	14	15	16	17	18
19	20	21	22	23	24	25
26	27	28	29	30		

TO DO THIS WEEK

APPOINTMENTS & ASSIGNMENTS	GENERAL STUDY	THE REST OF YOUR LIFE
Monday, May 30 *Memorial Day (U.S.), ● New Moon*		
Tuesday, May 31		
Wednesday, June 1		

THE ORIGINAL STUDENT CALENDAR

TO DO THIS MONTH

There are two ways to get enough. One is to continue to accumulate more and more. The other is to desire less.

— *G.K. Chesterton*

APPOINTMENTS & ASSIGNMENTS	GENERAL STUDY	THE REST OF YOUR LIFE
Thursday, June 2		
Friday, June 3		

Saturday, June 4	Sunday, June 5

THE ORIGINAL STUDENT CALENDAR

JUNE 2022

S	M	T	W	T	F	S
			1	2	3	4
5	**6**	**7**	**8**	**9**	**10**	**11**
12	13	14	15	16	17	18
19	20	21	22	23	24	25
26	27	28	29	30		

TO DO THIS WEEK

APPOINTMENTS & ASSIGNMENTS	GENERAL STUDY	THE REST OF YOUR LIFE
Monday, June 6		
Tuesday, June 7		
Wednesday, June 8		

CANADIAN MAIL ORDERS (U.S. & International orders on next page)

If you have difficulty finding the calendar, we'd be happy to fill your order. Mail this form or phone and pay by Visa or MasterCard, or order online at www.polestarcalendars.com.

For information on other Polestar calendars please visit our website www.polestarcalendars.com

Please Note: Calendars will be ready to ship in early June.

So, if you live in BC the cost for one calendar is $20.88

If you live in ON, one calendar is $21.41

If you live in NS,PE, NB, or NL, one calendar is $21.79

Anywhere else in Canada one calendar is $19.90

Visa/MasterCard payments:

Acct. #

_ _ _ _   _ _ _ _   _ _ _ _   _ _ _ _

Exp. _ _ / _ _ CVV _ _ _

Name ____________________

Please make your cheque/money order payable in Canadian funds to:

Polestar Calendars Ltd.,
6518 Slocan River Road,
Winlaw, B.C. V0G 2J0
Phone 1-800-296-6955

THE ORIGINAL STUDENT CALENDAR

____ copy/copies	*Aug. 2022– Aug. 2023 @ $13.95 each* (For orders of 3 or more = $12.00/copy)	________
Postage & Handling	$5.00 for each copy	________
	Subtotal	________
Tax payable on Subtotal, please select the sales tax that applies:	**Tax payable**	________

GST: 5% (AB, SK, MB, QC, YT, NT, NU)
GST: 5% / PST: 7% (BC residents only – GST/PST due on calendar, GST due on postage)
HST: 13% (ON)
HST: 15% (NS, PE, NB, NL)

Total Enclosed ________

Send calendars to: *(please print)*

Name ________________________________

Address ________________________________

City ____________ Province ____________ Postal Code ________

Email: ____________________ Phone ____________

American and International customers, please use order form on next page. Thanks!

AMERICAN AND INTERNATIONAL (Canadian orders on previous page)

If you have difficulty finding the calendar, we'd be happy to fill your order. Mail this form or phone and pay by Visa or MasterCard, or order online at www.polestarcalendars.com.

For information on other Polestar calendars please visit our website www.polestarcalendars.com

Please Note: Calendars will be ready to ship in early June.

Total American Funds Payment Info

# copies	*U.S.*	*International*
1 copy	20.45	28.95
2 copies	40.90	57.90
3 copies	55.50	81.00

Visa/MasterCard payments:

Acct. #

_ _ _ _   _ _ _ _   _ _ _ _   _ _ _ _

Exp. _ _ / _ _ CVV _ _ _

Name ____________________________

Please make your check/money order payable in U.S. funds to:

Polestar Calendars Ltd.,
6518 Slocan River Road,
Winlaw, B.C. Canada V0G 2J0
Phone 1-800-296-6955 (U.S. and Canada)
Phone 250-226-7670

THE ORIGINAL STUDENT CALENDAR

___ copy/copies *Aug. 2022 – Aug. 2023 @ $13.95 each* __________

(For orders of 3 or more = $12.00/copy)

Postage & Handling Charges to the U.S. = $7.50 for each copy __________

International = $16.00 for each copy __________

Total Enclosed __________

Send calendars to: *(please print)*

Name ____________________________

Address ____________________________

City ______________ State/Country ______________ Zip Code ________

Email: ______________________ Phone ______________

Canadian customers, please use order form on previous page. Thanks!

THE ORIGINAL STUDENT CALENDAR

TO DO THIS MONTH

Growing your own food is like printing your own money.

— *Ron Finley*

APPOINTMENTS & ASSIGNMENTS	GENERAL STUDY	THE REST OF YOUR LIFE
Thursday, June 9		
Friday, June 10		

Saturday, June 11	Sunday, June 12

THE ORIGINAL STUDENT CALENDAR

JUNE 2022

S	M	T	W	T	F	S
			1	2	3	4
5	6	7	8	9	10	11
12	**13**	**14**	**15**	**16**	**17**	**18**
19	20	21	22	23	24	25
26	27	28	29	30		

TO DO THIS WEEK

APPOINTMENTS & ASSIGNMENTS	GENERAL STUDY	THE REST OF YOUR LIFE
Monday, June 13		
Tuesday, June 14 ○ *Full Moon*		
Wednesday, June 15		

THE ORIGINAL STUDENT CALENDAR

TO DO THIS MONTH	
	The hardest thing is not doing what you want — it's knowing what you want. — *Naval Ravikant*

APPOINTMENTS & ASSIGNMENTS	GENERAL STUDY	THE REST OF YOUR LIFE
Thursday, June 16		
Friday, June 17		

Saturday, June 18	Sunday, June 19 *Father's Day (Canada, U.S.)*

THE ORIGINAL STUDENT CALENDAR

JUNE 2022

S	M	T	W	T	F	S
			1	2	3	4
5	6	7	8	9	10	11
12	13	14	15	16	17	18
19	**20**	**21**	**22**	**23**	**24**	**25**
26	27	28	29	30		

TO DO THIS WEEK

APPOINTMENTS & ASSIGNMENTS	GENERAL STUDY	THE REST OF YOUR LIFE
Monday, June 20		
Tuesday, June 21 *National Indigenous Peoples Day (Canada), Summer Solstice*		
Wednesday, June 22		

THE ORIGINAL STUDENT CALENDAR

TO DO THIS MONTH	
	Every encounter has within it the power of enchantment, if we're willing to look at it. — *Richard Wagamese*

APPOINTMENTS & ASSIGNMENTS	GENERAL STUDY	THE REST OF YOUR LIFE
Thursday, June 23		
Friday, June 24 *St. Jean Baptiste Day (Canada)*		

Saturday, June 25	Sunday, June 26

THE ORIGINAL STUDENT CALENDAR

JULY 2022

S	M	T	W	T	F	S
	27	28	29	30	**1**	**2**
3	**4**	5	6	7	8	9
10	11	12	13	14	15	16
17	18	19	20	21	22	23
24	25	26	27	28	29	30
31						

TO DO THIS WEEK

APPOINTMENTS & ASSIGNMENTS	GENERAL STUDY	THE REST OF YOUR LIFE
Monday, June 27		
Tuesday, June 28 ● *New Moon*		
Wednesday, June 29		

THE ORIGINAL STUDENT CALENDAR

TO DO THIS MONTH

Strawberries are the angels of the earth.

—*Jasmine Heiler*

APPOINTMENTS & ASSIGNMENTS	GENERAL STUDY	THE REST OF YOUR LIFE
Thursday, June 30		
Friday, July 1 *Canada Day*		

Saturday, July 2	Sunday, July 3

THE ORIGINAL STUDENT CALENDAR

JULY 2022						
S	M	T	W	T	F	S
					1	2
3	**4**	**5**	**6**	**7**	**8**	**9**
10	11	12	13	14	15	16
17	18	19	20	21	22	23
24	25	26	27	28	29	30
31						

TO DO THIS WEEK

APPOINTMENTS & ASSIGNMENTS	GENERAL STUDY	THE REST OF YOUR LIFE
Monday, July 4 *Independence Day (U.S.)*		
Tuesday, July 5		
Wednesday, July 6		

THE ORIGINAL STUDENT CALENDAR

TO DO THIS MONTH	It's summer, and time for wandering.... — *Kellie Elmore*

APPOINTMENTS & ASSIGNMENTS	GENERAL STUDY	THE REST OF YOUR LIFE
Thursday, July 7		
Friday, July 8		

Saturday, July 9	Sunday, July 10

THE ORIGINAL STUDENT CALENDAR

JULY 2022						
S	M	T	W	T	F	S
					1	2
3	**4**	5	6	7	8	9
10	**11**	**12**	**13**	**14**	**15**	**16**
17	18	19	20	21	22	23
24	25	26	27	28	29	30
31						

TO DO THIS WEEK

APPOINTMENTS & ASSIGNMENTS	GENERAL STUDY	THE REST OF YOUR LIFE
Monday, July 11		
Tuesday, July 12		
Wednesday, July 13 ○ *Full Moon*		

THE ORIGINAL STUDENT CALENDAR

TO DO THIS MONTH

I think the next best thing to solving a problem is finding some humour in it.

— *Glen Clark*

APPOINTMENTS & ASSIGNMENTS	GENERAL STUDY	THE REST OF YOUR LIFE
Thursday, July 14		
Friday, July 15		

Saturday, July 16	Sunday, July 17

THE ORIGINAL STUDENT CALENDAR

JULY 2022							TO DO THIS WEEK
S	**M**	**T**	**W**	**T**	**F**	**S**	
					1	2	
3	**4**	5	6	7	8	9	
10	11	12	13	14	15	16	
17	**18**	**19**	**20**	**21**	**22**	**23**	
24	25	26	27	28	29	30	
31							

APPOINTMENTS & ASSIGNMENTS	GENERAL STUDY	THE REST OF YOUR LIFE
Monday, July 18		
Tuesday, July 19		
Wednesday, July 20		

THE ORIGINAL STUDENT CALENDAR

TO DO THIS MONTH	Sometimes it's better not to think, and just to feel, when you're being creative. — *Beau Dick*

APPOINTMENTS & ASSIGNMENTS	GENERAL STUDY	THE REST OF YOUR LIFE
Thursday, July 21		
Friday, July 22		

Saturday, July 23	Sunday, July 24

THE ORIGINAL STUDENT CALENDAR

JULY 2022

S	M	T	W	T	F	S
					1	2
3	**4**	5	6	7	8	9
10	11	12	13	14	15	16
17	18	19	20	21	22	23
24	**25**	**26**	**27**	**28**	**29**	**30**
31						

TO DO THIS WEEK

APPOINTMENTS & ASSIGNMENTS	GENERAL STUDY	THE REST OF YOUR LIFE
Monday, July 25		
Tuesday, July 26		
Wednesday, July 27		

THE ORIGINAL STUDENT CALENDAR

TO DO THIS MONTH

Rest is not idleness, and to lie sometimes on the grass under the trees on a summer's day listening to the murmur of the water, or watching the clouds float across the sky, is hardly a waste of time.

— *Sir John Lubbock*

APPOINTMENTS & ASSIGNMENTS	GENERAL STUDY	THE REST OF YOUR LIFE
Thursday, July 28 ● *New Moon*		
Friday, July 29		

Saturday, July 30	Sunday, July 31

THE ORIGINAL STUDENT CALENDAR

AUGUST 2022

S	M	T	W	T	F	S
	1	2	3	4	5	6
7	8	9	10	11	12	13
14	15	16	17	18	19	20
21	22	23	24	25	26	27
28	29	30	31			

TO DO THIS WEEK

APPOINTMENTS & ASSIGNMENTS	GENERAL STUDY	THE REST OF YOUR LIFE
Monday, Aug. 1 *Civic Holiday (Canada)*		
Tuesday, Aug. 2		
Wednesday, Aug. 3		

THE ORIGINAL STUDENT CALENDAR

TO DO THIS MONTH

Here's to books — the cheapest vacation you can buy.

— *Charlaine Harris*

APPOINTMENTS & ASSIGNMENTS	GENERAL STUDY	THE REST OF YOUR LIFE
Thursday, Aug. 4		
Friday, Aug. 5		

Saturday, Aug. 6	Sunday, Aug. 7

THE ORIGINAL STUDENT CALENDAR

AUGUST 2022

S	M	T	W	T	F	S
	1	2	3	4	5	6
7	**8**	**9**	**10**	**11**	**12**	**13**
14	15	16	17	18	19	20
21	22	23	24	25	26	27
28	29	30	31			

TO DO THIS WEEK

APPOINTMENTS & ASSIGNMENTS	GENERAL STUDY	THE REST OF YOUR LIFE
Monday, Aug. 8		
Tuesday, Aug. 9		
Wednesday, Aug. 10		

THE ORIGINAL STUDENT CALENDAR

TO DO THIS MONTH	
	Pay attention to your vibes and trust your gut. We are all born with intuition.
	— *Jen Mazur*

APPOINTMENTS & ASSIGNMENTS	GENERAL STUDY	THE REST OF YOUR LIFE
Thursday, Aug. 11 ○ *Full Moon*		
Friday, Aug. 12		

Saturday, Aug. 13	Sunday, Aug. 14

THE ORIGINAL STUDENT CALENDAR

AUGUST 2022

S	M	T	W	T	F	S
	1	2	3	4	5	6
7	8	9	10	11	12	13
14	**15**	**16**	**17**	**18**	**19**	**20**
21	22	23	24	25	26	27
28	29	30	31			

TO DO THIS WEEK

APPOINTMENTS & ASSIGNMENTS	GENERAL STUDY	THE REST OF YOUR LIFE
Monday, Aug. 15		
Tuesday, Aug. 16		
Wednesday, Aug. 17		

THE ORIGINAL STUDENT CALENDAR

TO DO THIS MONTH	
	When the sun goes down and you look back on the day, go easy on yourself. A little self-forgiveness goes a long way. — *Austin Kleon*

APPOINTMENTS & ASSIGNMENTS	GENERAL STUDY	THE REST OF YOUR LIFE
Thursday, Aug. 18		
Friday, Aug. 19		

Saturday, Aug. 20	Sunday, Aug. 21

THE ORIGINAL STUDENT CALENDAR

AUGUST 2022

S	M	T	W	T	F	S
	1	2	3	4	5	6
7	8	9	10	11	12	13
14	15	16	17	18	19	20
21	**22**	**23**	**24**	**25**	**26**	**27**
28	29	30	31			

TO DO THIS WEEK

APPOINTMENTS & ASSIGNMENTS	GENERAL STUDY	THE REST OF YOUR LIFE
Monday, Aug. 22		
Tuesday, Aug. 23		
Wednesday, Aug. 24		

THE ORIGINAL STUDENT CALENDAR

TO DO THIS MONTH

If you don't act now while it's fresh in your mind, it will probably join the list of things you were always going to do but never quite got around to.

— *Paul Clitheroe*

APPOINTMENTS & ASSIGNMENTS	GENERAL STUDY	THE REST OF YOUR LIFE
Thursday, Aug. 25		
Friday, Aug. 26		

Saturday, Aug. 27 ● *New Moon*

Sunday, Aug. 28

THE ORIGINAL STUDENT CALENDAR

SEPTEMBER 2022

S	M	T	W	T	F	S
	29	30	31	**1**	**2**	**3**
4	**5**	6	7	8	9	10
11	12	13	14	15	16	17
18	19	20	21	22	23	24
25	26	27	28	29	30	

TO DO THIS WEEK

APPOINTMENTS & ASSIGNMENTS	GENERAL STUDY	THE REST OF YOUR LIFE
Monday, Aug. 29		
Tuesday, Aug. 30		
Wednesday, Aug. 31		

THE ORIGINAL STUDENT CALENDAR

TO DO THIS MONTH	
	Hope, at the end of the day, connects us all, no matter how different we are. — *Marketa Irglova*

APPOINTMENTS & ASSIGNMENTS	GENERAL STUDY	THE REST OF YOUR LIFE
Thursday, Sept. 1		
Friday, Sept. 2		

Saturday, Sept. 3	Sunday, Sept. 4

SEPTEMBER 2022 **THE ORIGINAL STUDENT CALENDAR** **SEPTEMBER 2022**

Sunday	Monday	Tuesday	Wednesday	Thursday	Friday	Saturday
				1	2	3
4	5 *Labour Day*	6	7	8	9	10 ○ *Full Moon*
11	12	13	14	15	16	17
18	19	20	21 *U.N. International Day of Peace*	22 *Autumnal Equinox*	23	24
25 ● *New Moon*	26 *First day of Rosh Hashanah*	27	28	29	30	

2022

SEPTEMBER

S	M	T	W	T	F	S
				1	2	3
4	**5**	6	7	8	9	10
11	12	13	14	15	16	17
18	19	20	21	22	23	24
25	26	27	28	29	30	

OCTOBER

S	M	T	W	T	F	S
						1
2	3	4	5	6	7	8
9	**10**	11	12	13	14	15
16	17	18	19	20	21	22
23	24	25	26	27	28	29
30	31					

NOVEMBER

S	M	T	W	T	F	S
		1	2	3	4	5
6	7	8	9	10	**11**	12
13	14	15	16	17	18	19
20	21	22	23	**24**	25	26
27	28	29	30			

DECEMBER

S	M	T	W	T	F	S
				1	2	3
4	5	6	7	8	9	10
11	12	13	14	15	16	17
18	19	20	21	22	23	24
25	**26**	27	28	29	30	31

2023

JANUARY

S	M	T	W	T	F	S
1	2	3	4	5	6	7
8	9	10	11	12	13	14
15	16	17	18	19	20	21
22	23	24	25	26	27	28
29	30	31				

FEBRUARY

S	M	T	W	T	F	S
			1	2	3	4
5	6	7	8	9	10	11
12	13	14	15	16	17	18
19	**20**	21	22	23	24	25
26	27	28				

MARCH

S	M	T	W	T	F	S
			1	2	3	4
5	6	7	8	9	10	11
12	13	14	15	16	17	18
19	20	21	22	23	24	25
26	27	28	29	30	31	

APRIL

S	M	T	W	T	F	S
						1
2	3	4	5	6	**7**	8
9	10	11	12	13	14	15
16	17	18	19	20	21	22
23	24	25	26	27	28	29
30						

MAY

S	M	T	W	T	F	S
	1	2	3	4	5	6
7	8	9	10	11	12	13
14	15	16	17	18	19	20
21	**22**	23	24	25	26	27
28	**29**	30	31			

JUNE

S	M	T	W	T	F	S
				1	2	3
4	5	6	7	8	9	10
11	12	13	14	15	16	17
18	19	20	21	22	23	24
25	26	27	28	29	30	

JULY

S	M	T	W	T	F	S
						1
2	3	**4**	5	6	7	8
9	10	11	12	13	14	15
16	17	18	19	20	21	22
23	24	25	26	27	28	29
30	31					

AUGUST

S	M	T	W	T	F	S
		1	2	3	4	5
6	**7**	8	9	10	11	12
13	14	15	16	17	18	19
20	21	22	23	24	25	26
27	28	29	30	31		

SEPTEMBER

S	M	T	W	T	F	S
					1	2
3	**4**	5	6	7	8	9
10	11	12	13	14	15	16
17	18	19	20	21	22	23
24	25	26	27	28	29	30

AUGUST EXPENSES

AUG. 2021	BOOKS & COURSE EXP.	RENT	TRANSPORT-ATION	FOOD & FUN STUFF	MISC.	TOTAL
1						
2						
3						
4						
5						
6						
7						
8						
9						
10						
11						
12						
13						
14						
15						
16						
17						
18						
19						
20						
21						
22						
23						
24						
25						
26						
27						
28						
29						
30						
31						

MONTHLY TOTAL ____________

SEPTEMBER EXPENSES

SEPT. 2021	BOOKS & COURSE EXP.	RENT	TRANSPORT-ATION	FOOD & FUN STUFF	MISC.	TOTAL
1						
2						
3						
4						
5						
6						
7						
8						
9						
10						
11						
12						
13						
14						
15						
16						
17						
18						
19						
20						
21						
22						
23						
24						
25						
26						
27						
28						
29						
30						

MONTHLY TOTAL ______

OCTOBER EXPENSES

OCT. 2021	BOOKS & COURSE EXP.	RENT	TRANSPORT-ATION	FOOD & FUN STUFF	MISC.	TOTAL
1						
2						
3						
4						
5						
6						
7						
8						
9						
10						
11						
12						
13						
14						
15						
16						
17						
18						
19						
20						
21						
22						
23						
24						
25						
26						
27						
28						
29						
30						
31						

MONTHLY TOTAL

NOVEMBER EXPENSES

NOV. 2021	BOOKS & COURSE EXP.	RENT	TRANSPORT-ATION	FOOD & FUN STUFF	MISC.	TOTAL
1						
2						
3						
4						
5						
6						
7						
8						
9						
10						
11						
12						
13						
14						
15						
16						
17						
18						
19						
20						
21						
22						
23						
24						
25						
26						
27						
28						
29						
30						

MONTHLY TOTAL ____________

DECEMBER EXPENSES

DEC. 2021	BOOKS & COURSE EXP.	RENT	TRANSPORT-ATION	FOOD & FUN STUFF	MISC.	TOTAL
1						
2						
3						
4						
5						
6						
7						
8						
9						
10						
11						
12						
13						
14						
15						
16						
17						
18						
19						
20						
21						
22						
23						
24						
25						
26						
27						
28						
29						
30						
31						

MONTHLY TOTAL ____________

JANUARY EXPENSES

JAN. 2022	BOOKS & COURSE EXP.	RENT	TRANSPORT-ATION	FOOD & FUN STUFF	MISC.	TOTAL
1						
2						
3						
4						
5						
6						
7						
8						
9						
10						
11						
12						
13						
14						
15						
16						
17						
18						
19						
20						
21						
22						
23						
24						
25						
26						
27						
28						
29						
30						
31						

MONTHLY TOTAL ______

FEBRUARY EXPENSES

FEB. 2022	BOOKS & COURSE EXP.	RENT	TRANSPORT-ATION	FOOD & FUN STUFF	MISC.	TOTAL
1						
2						
3						
4						
5						
6						
7						
8						
9						
10						
11						
12						
13						
14						
15						
16						
17						
18						
19						
20						
21						
22						
23						
24						
25						
26						
27						
28						

MONTHLY TOTAL ____________

MAR. 2022	BOOKS & COURSE EXP.	RENT	TRANSPORT-ATION	FOOD & FUN STUFF	MISC.	TOTAL
1						
2						
3						
4						
5						
6						
7						
8						
9						
10						
11						
12						
13						
14						
15						
16						
17						
18						
19						
20						
21						
22						
23						
24						
25						
26						
27						
28						
29						
30						
31						

MONTHLY TOTAL ____________

APRIL EXPENSES

APRIL 2022	BOOKS & COURSE EXP.	RENT	TRANSPORT-ATION	FOOD & FUN STUFF	MISC.	TOTAL
1						
2						
3						
4						
5						
6						
7						
8						
9						
10						
11						
12						
13						
14						
15						
16						
17						
18						
19						
20						
21						
22						
23						
24						
25						
26						
27						
28						
29						
30						

MONTHLY TOTAL ________

MAY 2022	BOOKS & COURSE EXP.	RENT	TRANSPORT-ATION	FOOD & FUN STUFF	MISC.	TOTAL
1						
2						
3						
4						
5						
6						
7						
8						
9						
10						
11						
12						
13						
14						
15						
16						
17						
18						
19						
20						
21						
22						
23						
24						
25						
26						
27						
28						
29						
30						
31						

MONTHLY TOTAL ______

JUNE EXPENSES

JUNE 2022	BOOKS & COURSE EXP.	RENT	TRANSPORT-ATION	FOOD & FUN STUFF	MISC.	TOTAL
1						
2						
3						
4						
5						
6						
7						
8						
9						
10						
11						
12						
13						
14						
15						
16						
17						
18						
19						
20						
21						
22						
23						
24						
25						
26						
27						
28						
29						
30						

MONTHLY TOTAL ________

JULY EXPENSES

JULY 2022	BOOKS & COURSE EXP.	RENT	TRANSPORT-ATION	FOOD & FUN STUFF	MISC.	TOTAL
1						
2						
3						
4						
5						
6						
7						
8						
9						
10						
11						
12						
13						
14						
15						
16						
17						
18						
19						
20						
21						
22						
23						
24						
25						
26						
27						
28						
29						
30						
31						

MONTHLY TOTAL ______

AUGUST EXPENSES

AUG. 2021	BOOKS & COURSE EXP.	RENT	TRANSPORT-ATION	FOOD & FUN STUFF	MISC.	TOTAL
1						
2						
3						
4						
5						
6						
7						
8						
9						
10						
11						
12						
13						
14						
15						
16						
17						
18						
19						
20						
21						
22						
23						
24						
25						
26						
27						
28						
29						
30						
31						

MONTHLY TOTAL ______

Notes

Notes

Notes

Notes

Notes

THE ORIGINAL STUDENT CALENDAR

Name	*Phone/email*	*Address*

THE ORIGINAL STUDENT CALENDAR

Name	Phone/email	Address

THE ORIGINAL STUDENT CALENDAR

Name	*Phone/email*	*Address*